We're Going on a Picnic

Gerald Rose

CAMBRIDGE
UNIVERSITY PRESS

It was a fine day for a picnic.

"Why don't you want to come, Gran?" asked Dan.

"You'll see," smiled Gran as she waved them off.

Dad drove the car into a field and they all got out.

"Mud!" shouted Dan. "Great!"

"Let's have the picnic," said Mum.
They began to eat.
But then . . . CLOP, CLOP, CLOP.
"Look," said Vicky. "A horse."

Vicky loved horses . . . but not this one! It ate her bun.

"SHOO!" said Vicky. "Go away."

But the horse wouldn't go away.

"We'll have to find another field," said Mum.

They packed up the picnic and ran into the next field.

"Now we can have the picnic," said Mum.
But then . . . BAA, BAA, BAA.
"Sheep!" said Dan.

There were sheep everywhere.
"SHOO!" shouted Dan.

But the sheep wouldn't go away.
"We'll have to find another field," said Dad.
They packed up the picnic again and ran.

They stopped to have a rest.
"*Now* we can have the picnic," said Dad.
But then . . . WOOF, WOOF, WOOF.

"Sheep-dogs!" shouted Dan. "Help!"
"Look, there's a river," said Dad. "And a boat. Come on, run!"

They jumped into the boat.
"Just in time," said Mum.
Dad rowed the boat down the river.

"Now we can have the picnic here," said Mum.

But then . . . QUACK, QUACK, QUACK.
"Ducks!" shouted Vicky.
There were ducks everywhere.

Then a swan swam up. It tried to grab a bun from Vicky's hand. She jumped back and . . . SPLASH! Vicky fell into the water.

"HELP!" she yelled.

"I'll save her," said Dad, and he jumped in.
"I'll save her," said Mum, and she jumped in.

Dan got so excited he just fell in.

There was a lot of splashing about before they got to the river bank.

"Let's go home," said Mum.

They walked back to the car.
But the car was . . . STUCK IN THE MUD!
Mum got in the car and shouted, "PUSH!"

They pushed and pushed until . . . SPLAT!
Mud went everywhere.

21

At last they got the car out and drove off.
"No more picnics for us," said Dad.

When they got home, Gran said, "You poor things. You go and clean up. Then I've got a surprise for you."

Gran took them into the garden. She had made them a PICNIC!

"Home is the best place for a picnic," said Gran.